Regarding Views and Regime Changes

Regarding Views and Regime Changes

Yeshe Tsogyal

Main Translator: Sir John Woodroffe

Assistant Translator: Kazi Dawa-samdup

Inter-Tale Annotator: Sir John Woodroffe

The translation by Sir John Woodroffe and Kazi Dawa-samdup featured an introduction segueing into an edited tale with occasional annotations, and it became transfigured into the centerpiece of this work.

This edition includes a lightly-copy-edited-and-redacted, reformatted transcription of nearly all of the "Matam Rutra (The Right and Wrong Interpretation)" chapter of *Shakti and Shakta* (1918). After that, it features a set of post-tale annotations, several of which consist of strategically-sequenced repurposed quotes by Lao-Tzu as translated by James Legge, carefully repurposed quotes by Anonymous/Unknown as translated by F. Max Müller, and newly-generated quotes by Synapsid Revelations Press.

Post-Tale Annotator: Synapsid Revelations Press

Providers of Supplemental Quotations included Post-Tale:
Lao-Tzu, Anonymous/Unknown, and Synapsid Revelations Press

Translators of Supplemental Quotations, Where Applicable:
James Legge and F. Max Müller

Composite Editor, Copy Editor, and Publisher:
Synapsid Revelations Press

Regarding Views and Regime Changes

Yes-shes-mtso-rgyal (also known as Yeshe Tsogyal), circa 8th Century
ISBN: 978-1-963470-17-8
Supplemental Literary Providers: various contributors, various periods

Synapsid Revelations Press Corporation
9619 Meadowcroft Drive
Houston, Texas, 77063, United States of America
Date of Publication: December 22, 2024 (between a Solstice & a Festivus)

Consider this literally, metaphorically, and/or parabolically, if so chosen.

The centerpiece item here consists of the second-through-ultimate paragraphs of the "Matam Rudra (The Right and Wrong Interpretation)" chapter of *Shakti and Shakta* (1918) by Arthur Avalon / Sir John Woodroffe.

Yeshe Tsogyal authored most of that, and Woodroffe weaved together an introduction that segues into the main storytelling. Woodroffe also inserted brief annotations at several choice junctures. Those interzonal annotations often appear parenthetically.

In this case Tsogyal receives full credit as the author of this literary work, which includes supplemental portions from several additional contributors.

REGARDING VIEWS AND REGIME CHANGES

Guru Padmasambhava, a vital male founder of "Lamaism," had five female disciples who compiled several accounts of the teachings of their Master and hid them in various places for the benefit of future believers. One disciple—Khandro Yeshe Tsogyal—was a Tibetan lady whom some said to have possessed such a wonderful power of memory that if she was told a thing only once she remembered it forever. She gathered what she had heard from her Guru into a book called the Padma Thangyig Serteng or Golden Rosary of the history of her Guru who was entitled the Lotus-born (Padmasambhava). The book was hidden away and subsequently, under inspiration, revealed Mid-Second-Millennium Common Era by a Terton.

The first Chapter of the work deals with Sukhavati, the realm of Buddha Amitabha. In the second the Buddha emanates a ray which is incarnated for the welfare of the Universe. In Chapter III it is said that there have been a Buddha and a Guru working together in various worlds and at various times, the former preaching the Sutras and the latter the Tantras. The fourth Chapter speaks of the Mantras and the five Dhyani Buddhas (as to which see *Shri-cakra-sambhara Tantra),* and in the fifth we find the subject of the present Chapter, an account of the origin of the Vajrayana Faith. The present Chapter is based on a translation, which I asked Kazi Dawa-samdup to prepare for me, of portions of the Thangyig Serteng. I have further had, and here acknowledge, the assistance of the very learned Lama Ugyen Tanzin, in the elucidation of the inner meaning of the legend. I cannot go fully into this but give certain indications which will enable the competent to work out much of the rest for themselves from the terrible symbolism in which evil for evil's sake is here expressed.

The story is that of the rise and fall of the Self. The disciple "Transcendent Faith" who became the Bodhisattva Vajrapani illustrates the former; the case of "Black Salvation" who incarnated as a Demoniac Rutra displays the latter. He was no ordinary man, for at the time of his initiation he had already attained eight out of the thirteen stages (Bhumika) on the way to perfect Buddhahood. His powers were correspondingly great. But the higher the rise the greater the fall if it comes. Through misunderstanding and misapplying, as so many others have done, the Tantrik doctrine, he "fell back" into Hell. Extraordinary men who were teachers of recondite doctrines such as those of Thubka, who was himself "hard to overcome," seem not to have failed to warn lesser brethren against their dangers. It is commonly said in Tibet of the so-called "heroic" modes of extremist Yoga, that they waft the disciple with the utmost speed either to the heights of Nirvana or to the depths of Hell. For the aspirant is compared to a snake which is made to go up a hollow bamboo. It must ascend and escape at the top, at the peril otherwise of falling down.

Notwithstanding these warnings many of the vulgar, the vicious, the misunderstanding and the fools who play with fire have gone to Hells far more terrible than those which await human frailties in pursuance of the common life of men whose progress if slow is sure. "Black Salvation", though an advanced disciple, misinterpreted his teacher's doctrine and consciously identifying himself with the world-evil fell into Hell. In time he rose therefrom and incarnating at first, in gross material forms, he at length manifested as a great Rutra, the embodiment of all wickedness. The Tibetan Rutra here spoken of and the Indian Rutra seem to be etymologically equivalent, but their meaning is different. Both are fierce and terrible Spirits; but a Rutra as here depicted is essentially evil, and neither the Lord of any sensual celestial paradise, nor the Cosmic Shakti which loosens forms. A Rutra is rather what in some secret circles is called (though in ungrammatical Sanskrit) an Adhatma, or a soul upon the lower and destructive path. The general destructive energy (Samhara-Shakti), however, uses for its purpose the disintegrating propensities of these forms. The evil which appears as Rutra is the expression of various kinds of Egoism. Thus Matam Rutra is Egoism as attached to the gross physical body. Again, all sentient worldly being gives expression to its feelings, saying "I am happy, unhappy, and so forth." All this is here embodied in the speech of the Rutra and is called Akar Rutra. Khatram Rutra is Egoism of the mind, as when it is said of any object "this is mine". "Black Salvation" became a Rutra of such terrific power that to save him and the world the Buddhas intervened. There are four methods by which they and the Bodhisattvas subdue and save sentient being, namely, the Peaceful, the Grand or Attractive, the Fascinating which renders powerless (Vasikaranam), and the stern method of downright Force. All forms of Egoism must be destroyed in order that the pure "That Which Is" or formless Consciousness may be attained. "Black Salvation" incarnated as the Pride of Egoism in its most terrible form. And, in order to subdue him, the last two methods had to be employed. He was, through the Glorious One, redeemed by the suffering which attends all sin and became the "Dark Defender of the Faith," which by his egoistic apostasy he had abjured, to be later the Buddha known as the "Lord of Ashes" in that world which is called "the immediately self-produced."

How this came about the legend describes.

* * * * * * * * * * * *

The fifth Chapter of the Golden Rosary says that Guru Padma-Vajradhara was reborn as Bhikshu Thubkazhonnu, which means the "youth who is hard to overcome". He was a Tantrik who preached an abstruse doctrine which is condensed in the following verse:

"He who has attained the 'That Which Is'
Or uncreated In-itself-ness
Is unaffected even by the 'four things'
Just as the cloud which floats in the sky
Adheres not thereto.
This is the way of Supreme Yoga.
Than this in all the three worlds
There is not a higher wisdom."

* * * * *

This Guru had two disciples, Kuntri and his servant Pramadeva. To the latter was given, on initiation, the name "Transcendent Faith," and to the former "Black Salvation". This last name was a prophetic prediction that he would be saved, not through peaceful or agreeable means but through the just wrath of the Jinas. The real meaning of the verse as understood and practiced by Pramadeva and as declared to be right by the Guru was as follows:

"The pure Consciousness (Dagpa-ye-shes) is the foundation (Gshihdsin) of the limited consciousness (Rnam-shes) and is in Scripture "That which is," the real uncreated "In-Itself-ness". This being unaffected or unruffled is the path of Tantra. Passions (Klesha) are like clouds wandering in the wide spaces of the sky. (These clouds are distinct from, and do not touch the back-ground of space against which they appear.) So passions do not touch but disappear from the Void (Shunyata). Whilst ascending upwards the threefold accomplishment (Activity, non-activity, absolute repose) must be persevered in; and this is the meaning of our Teacher Thubka's doctrine."

The latter, however, was misunderstood by "Black Salvation" (Tharpa Nagpo) who took it to mean that he was to make no effort to save himself by the gaining of merit, but that he was to indulge in the four acts of sinful enjoyment, by the eye, nose, tongue and organ of generation. On this account, he fell out with his brother in the faith Pramadeva, and later with his Guru, both of whom he caused to be persecuted and banished the country. Continuing in a career of reckless and sin-hardened life, he died unrepentant after a score of years passed in various diabolical practices. He fell

into Hell and continued there for countless ages. At the close of
the time of Buddha Dipankara (Marmedzad or "Light maker") he
was reborn several times as huge sea monsters. At length, just
before the time of the last Buddha Sakya Muni, he was born as
the son of a woman of loose morals in a country called Lankapuri
of the Rakshasas. This woman used to consort with three Spirits
— a Deva in the morning, a Fire Genius at noon, and a Daitya in
the evening. "Black Salvation" was reborn in the eighth month as
the offspring of these three Spirits. The child was a terrible
monster, black of color, with three heads, each of which had three
eyes, six hands, four feet and two wings. He was horrible to look
at, and immediately at his birth all the auspicious signs of the
country disappeared, and the eighteen inauspicious signs were
seen. Malignant epidemics attacked the whole region of Lankapuri. Some died, others only suffered, but all were in misery.
Lamentation, famine and sorrow beset the land. There were
disease, bloodshed, mildew, hailstorms, droughts, floods and all
other kinds of calamities. Even dreams were frightful, and
ominous signs portending a great catastrophe oppressed all. Evil
spirits roamed the land. So great were the evils that it seemed as
if the good merits of everyone had been exhausted all at once.

The mother who had given birth to this monster died nine days
after its birth. The people of the country decreed that this
monstrous infant should be bound to the mother's corpse and left
in the cemetery. The infant was then tied to his mother's breast.
The mother was borne away in a stretcher to the cemetery, and
the stretcher was left at the foot of a poisonous tree which had a

boar's den at its root, a poisonous snake coiled round the middle of its trunk, and a bird of prey sitting in its uppermost branches. (These animals are the emblems of lust, anger and greed respectively which "kindle the fire of individuality".) At this place there was a huge sepulcher built by the Rakshasas where they used to leave their dead at the foot of the tree. Elephants and tigers came there to die; serpents infested it, and witch-like spirits called Dakinis and Ghouls brought human bodies there. After the bearers of the corpse had left, the infant sustained his life by sucking the breasts of his mother's corpse. These yielded only a thin, watery fluid for seven days. Next, he sucked the blood to survive another week; then he gnawed at the breast and lived the third week; then he ate the entrails to make it another week. Then he ate the outer flesh and lived for the fifth week. Lastly, he crunched the bones, sucked the marrow, licked a variety of bodily fluids and brains, and lived yet another week. He in six weeks thus developed full physical maturity. Having exhausted his stock of food he moved about; and his motion shook the cemetery building to pieces. He observed the Ghouls and Dakinis feasting on human corpses which he took as his food and human blood as the drink, filling the skulls with it. His clothing was dried human skins as also the hides of dead elephants, the flesh of which he also ate. He ate also the flesh of tigers and wrapped his loins in their furs. He used serpents as bracelets, anklets, armlets and as necklaces and garlands. His lips were thick with frozen fat, and his body was covered with ashes from the burning ground. He wore a garland of dead skulls on one string; freshly severed heads on another; and decomposing heads on a third. These were worn crosswise as a triple garland. Each cheek was adorned with a spot of blood. His three great heads ever wrathful, of three different colors, were fierce and horrible to look at. The middle head was dark blue and those to the right and left were white and red respectively. His body and limbs which were of gigantic size and proportions were ashy gray. His skin was coarse and his hair as stiff as hog's bristles. His mouth wide agape showed fangs. His terrible eyes were fixed in a stare. Half of the dark brown hair on his head stood erect, bound with four kinds of snakes. The nails of his fingers and toes were like the talons of a great bird of prey, which seized hold of everything within reach, whether animals or human corpses which he crushed and swallowed. He bore a trident and other weapons in his right hands, and with his left he filled the emptied skulls with blood which he drank with great relish. He was a monster of ugliness who delighted in every kind of impious act. His unnatural food produced a strange luster on his face, which shone with a dull though great and terrible light. His breath was so poisonous that those touched by it were attacked with various diseases. For his nostrils breathed forth disease. His eyes, ears and arms produced the 404 different ills. Thus, the diseases paralysis, epilepsy, bubonic swellings, urinary ills, skin diseases, aches, rheumatism, gout, colic, cholera, leprosy, cancer, small-pox, dropsy and various other sores and boils appeared in this world at that time. (For evil thoughts and acts make the vital spirit sick and thence springs gross disease.)

The name of this great Demon was Matam Rutra. He was the fruit of the Karma of the great wickedness of his former life as Tharpa Nagpo. At that time, in each of the 24 Pilgrimages, there was a powerful destructive Bhairava Spirit. These Devas, Gandharvas, Rakshasas, Asuras and Nagas were proud, malignant and mighty Spirits, despotic masters of men, with great magical powers of illusion and transformation. These Spirits used to wander over these countries dressed in the eight sepulchral raiments, wearing the six kinds of bone ornaments, and armed with various weapons, accompanied by their female consorts, and reveled in all kinds of obscene orgies. Their chief occupation consisted in depriving all sentient beings of their lives. After consultation, all these Spirits elected Matam Rutra as their Chief. Thus all these non-human beings became his slaves. In the midst of his horrible retinue he continued to devour human beings alive until the race became almost destroyed and the cities emptied. He was thus the terrible scourge that the earth had ever seen. All who died in those days fell into Hell. But, as for Matam Rutra himself, his pride knew no bounds: he thought there was no one greater than himself and would roar out:

"Who is there greater and mightier than I? If there be any Lord who would excel me, Him too will I subjugate."

As there was no one to gainsay him, the world was oppressed by heavy gloom. At that time, however, Kali proclaimed,

"In the country of Lanka, the land of Rakshasas,
In a portion of the city called Koka-Thangmaling,

On the peak of Malaya, the abode of Thunder,

There dwells the Lord of Lanka, King of Rakshasas.

He is a disciple of the light-giving Buddha.

His fame far excels thine.

He is unconquerable in fight by any foe.

He sleeps secure and doth awake in peace."

Hearing this, the pride and ambition of the Demon became aflame. His body emitted flames great enough to have consumed all worlds at the great Kalpa dissolution. His voice resounded in a deep thundering roar like that of a thousand clasp of thunder heard together. With sparks of fire flying from his mouth he summoned a huge force. He filled the very heavens with them, and moving with the speed of a meteor he invaded the Rakshasa's capital of Koka-Thangmaling. Encamping, Matam Rutra proclaimed his name proudly, at which the entire country of Lanka trembled and was shaken terribly as though by an earthquake. The Rakshasas, both male and female, became terrified. The King of the Rakshasas sent spies to find out the cause of these happenings. They went and saw the terrible force, and being terrified at the sight reported the fearful news to their king. He sat in Samadhi for a while, and divined the following: According to the Sutra of King Gunadhara it was said, "One who has vexed his Guru's heart, and broken his friend and brother's heart: the haughty son, being released from the three Hells, will take rebirth here, and he will surely conquer the Lord of Lanka.

"In the end, he will be conquered by many Sugatas (the blissful ones, or Buddhas). And this event will give birth to the Anuttara-Vajrayana Faith." The Buddha Marmedzad having revealed the event, he wished to see whether this was the Matam Rutra Demon referred to in the prophesy. So he collected a force of Rakshasas and went forth to fight a battle with the Demon force.

*   *   *   *   *

Matam Rutra was very angry and said:

"I am the Great Invincible One, who is without a peer,
I am the Ishvara Mahadeva.
The four great Kings of the four quarters are my vassals,
The eight different tribes of Spirits are my slaves,
I am the Lord of the whole World.
Who is going to withstand and confront me?
Tutra, Matra, Marutra."

With this battle cry he overcame the forces of the Rakshasas. Then the King of the Rakshasas and all his forces submitted to the King of the Demons, saying "I repent me of my attempt to withstand you, in the hope of upholding the Faith of the Buddhas, and to spread it far and wide. I now submit to you and become your loyal subject. I will not rebel against you." When he had thus overcome the Rakshasas, he assumed the title of Matamka, the Chief of all the Rakshasas. His pride increased, and he proclaimed, "Who is there greater than I'?"

Then, Kali again cleverly excited his ambition and pride by saying, "The Chief of the armies of the Asuras (Lhamin that is "not Devas"), named Mahakaru, is mightier than you."

Thereupon he invaded the realms of the Asuras, with his demon force, and all the Asuras becoming affected with various terrible maladies were powerless to resist him. The Rutra caught hold of the Asura King by the leg and whirling him thrice round his head flung him into the Jambudvipa where he fell in a place called the Ge-ne-gynad, meaning the place of eight merits. Then those of the Asuras who had not been killed, the eight planets (Grahas) and the twenty-eight constellations (Nakshatras) and their hosts sought refuge in every direction, but failing to obtain safety anywhere, they returned and surrendered themselves to the Demon Matam Rutra. Then the Asuras guided the Rutra and his forces to a Palace named the Globular Palace like a skull where they established their Capital. In the center of this Palace, the Rutra hoisted his banner of Victory. They arranged their dreadful weapons by the side of the entrance, and the place was surrounded by numerous followers with magical powers.

Having thus shown his own great magical powers, he took up the King of Mountains, Meru, upon the tip of his finger and whirling it round his head, he proclaimed these boastful words, "Rutra, Matra, Marutra, who is there in this universe greater than myself? In all the three Lokas, there is none greater than I. And if there be any, him also will I subdue."

To these boastful words Kali answered,

"In the thirty-third Deva-Loka and in the happy
celestial regions of the Tushita Heavens,
Sitting amidst the golden assembly of disciples,
Is the Holy Savior of all beings, Regent of the Devas
(Dampa- Togkar).
Having been anointed, He is venerated and praised by
all the Deva Kings.
He summons all the Devas to his assembly by sounding
the various instruments of heavenly music
Accompanied by a celestial Chorus.
He is greater than yourself."

On her so saying, the Archdemon blazed forth into a fury of
pride and wrath, and set forth to conquer the Tushita Heavens.
The Bodhisattva (Dampa-Togkar) was sitting enthroned on a
throne of precious metals, in the midst of thousands of Devatas,
both male and female, and was preaching Dharma to them. The
Archdemon seized Dampa-Togkar from his throne, and threw him
down into this world-system. All the Devas and Devis there
gathered exclaimed, "Alas, what a fate, O, the sinful wretch!"
seven times over. Thereupon the Rutra fiercely said:

"Put on two cloths, and sit down on your seats, every one of you!
How can I be conquered by you? I am the mighty destroyer and
subjugator of all."

(The expression "Put on two cloths" was said by way of contempt
for the priestly robes which consist of three pieces, being a wrap-
per above, and one below and one over both. Dampa- Togkar is the

Bodhisattva who is coming as Buddha to teach in the human world. He descends from the Tushita Heavens where he reigns as Regent).

When the celestial Regent of the Tushita Heavens (Dampa-Togkar) was about to pass away from there, he uttered this prophesy to his disciples, who were around him: "Listen unto me, Ye my disciples: This apostate disciple, Tharpa-Nagpo (Black Salvation), Who does not believe in the Buddha's Doctrine, He is destined to pervert the Devas and Asuras, And to bend them to his yoke.

"He hates the perfect Buddha, and he will work much evil in this world-system.

"There are two, who can deprive him of his terrible power;

"They are Thubka-Zhonnu and Dad-Phags (Pramadeva, Arya Shraddha called Transcendent Faith).

"They will be able to make him taste the fruits of his evil deeds in this very life.

"He will not be subdued by peaceful, nor by any generous means.

"He will only be conquered by the methods of Fascination and Sternness."

(The various means of redemption have been previously explained. Thubka and his good disciple "Transcendent Faith" who had then become Buddha Vajra-Sattva, and Bodhisattva Vajra-pani were selected for this purpose. They assumed the forms of the Devatas with the Horse's head (Hayagriva) and the Sow's head (Vajra-Varahi).)

"Who, of the Noble Sangha, will doubt this, That Hayagriva and Vajra-Varahi will give him their bodies."

(When it is said 'These will give him their bodies' this means, as hereafter described, entering the Rutra's body, assuming his shape and destroying his Rutra life and nature. They give him their divine bodies so that they may destroy his demoniac body).

"And who will not trust in the Wisdom of the Jinas, to conquer him by the upward-piercing method, From this (demon) will come the Precious-nectar, which will be of use in acquiring Virtue. From this (demon) will originate the changing of poison into elixir. (There are various Tantrik methods suited to various natures.

"The upward-piercing" (Khatar-yar-phig) is that of Vajrayana. This is the method which goes upward and upward, that is straight upward without delay and without going to right or left. To change poison into nectar or elixir is a well-known principle of these schools. "This Demon will have to be ground down and destroyed to the last atom, in one body. (It is said 'in one body' because, ordinarily, several lives are necessary; but in this case and by this method Liberation is achieved in a single life-time and in one body. Not one atom of the Rutra body is left, for Egoism is wholly destroyed.)

"The Divine Horse-headed Deity (Vajra-Hayagriva), is he who will dispel this threatening misfortune, Dad-phags, (Pramadeva who was given on initiation the name 'Transcendent Faith') is at present Vajrapani (Bodhisattva).

"And Thubka-Zhonnu is, at present, the Buddha Vajrasattva.

"The divine prophesies of the Jinas are to be interpreted thus:
'They will exterminate their opponents.

"For myself I go to take birth in Maya-Devi's womb.

"I will practice Samadhi at the root of the Bodhi-Tree.

"I will not hold those beliefs in doubt.

"For it has been said that the Buddha's Faith will triumph over this,

"And will remain long in the Jambudvipa.

"By means of the mysterious practice of Emancipating by means of Communion.'"

(The practice here referred to is the method called Jordol (sByor sGrol) which has both exoteric and esoteric meanings, such as in the case of the latter the communion of the Divine Male and Female whose union destroys to its uttermost root egoistic attachment; the communion with Shunyata whose innermost significance is the non-dual Consciousness (gNyismed-yeshes) which dispels ignorance and cuts at the root of all Samsaric life by the destruction of all the Rutra forms. "Female" here is Sunyata and not a woman. When a learned Lama is asked why the terms of sex are used they say it is to symbolize Thabs (Upaya) and Shesrabs (Prajña) which it is not possible to further explain here (See *Mahanirvana Tantra* and *Kaulavali Nirnaya).)*

"The Matam Rutra, which is clinging to the body as 'I' will be dispelled, All forms of worldly happiness and pain, the Egoism of Speech (Akar Rutra), Will be destroyed.

"The saying 'this is mine' of anything, The mental 'I' (or Khatram-Rutra) is freed.

"The true nature and distinguishing attributes of a Rutra, Which is manifest outwardly, exists inwardly, and lies hidden secretly, In short all the fifty-eight Rutras, with their hosts, will be destroyed completely."

(I have already dealt with the meaning of the term, Rutra. Here the Egoisms of body, feelings, mind are referred to. The Glorious One will eradicate the physical and all other Rutras, the monster of the self in all its forms, gross, subtle and causal.)

"The world though deprived of happiness will rejoice again. The world will be filled with the Precious Dharma of the Tri-Ratna.

"The Righteous Faith has not declined, nor has it passed away."

(Thus did the Regent of the Tushita Heavens prophesy the advent of the Tantrik method for the complete destruction and the elimination of the demon of "Egotism" from the nature of the devotees on the path by means of Jordol.)

* * * * *

After uttering these prophecies, he passed away and took re-birth in the womb of Queen Maya Devi. Then the Archdemon, having subjugated all the Devas of the thirty-third and the Tushita Heavens, appointed the two Demons Mara and Devadatta, his two chief officers, to suppress Indra and Brahma. The Archdemon himself took up his abode in the Malaya Mountain, in the place called the Human skull-like Mansion. He used to feed upon Devas and human beings, both males and females. Drums, bells, cymbals and every kind of stringed and other musical instruments were played to him in a perpetual concert with songs and dances.

Every kind of enjoyment which the Devas used to enjoy, he enjoyed perpetually. (8th Chapter ends).

* * * * *

The 9th Chapter deals with the defeat and destruction of the Archdemon Matam Rutra by the Buddhas of the ten directions.

Then there assembled together Dharmakaya Buddha Samanta-bhadra (Chosku Kuntu Zangpo) and his attendants from the Wogmin (Akanishta) Heavens, from other Heavens, Sambhoga-kaya Vajradhara with his attendants; and Vajrapani Nirman-akaya with his attendants. In short, from the various heavens of the ten directions came the different Buddhas and Bodhisattvas. All held a consultation together and came to this resolution:

"Unless the power of the Buddhas be exerted to subjugate the Rutra, the Faith of the Buddhas will cease to spread and will degenerate. That body which has committed such violent outrages on every other being, must be made to suffer the agonies of being hurt by weapons, wielded by avengers. If he is not made to feel the consequences of his deeds, the Jinas who have proclaimed the Truth will be falsified. He is not to be destroyed but to be subdued." Having thus agreed, all the Buddhas began to seek with their omniscient eyes, him who was destined to conquer this Rutra. They saw that Thubka-Zhonnu who had attained the state of Buddha Vajrasattva and Dadphags who had become Vajrapani were to subdue him, and that the time was also ripe. So both of them came with their respective retinue and were blessed and endowed with Power by all the Buddhas, who gave these instructions. "Do ye assume the forms and sexes of Chenrezi and Dolma (Avalokita and Tara) and do ye subdue the Enemy by assuming the shapes of the Deities having the Horse-mane and the Sow's head (Haya-griva and Vajra-Varahi)."

(The latter is commonly known in English translations as the "Diamond Sow". Vajra is the Sanskrit equivalent of the word Dorje in Tibetan. The latter has many meanings; Indra's thunderbolt, the Lamas' scepter, diamond and so forth: and is in fact used of anything of a high and mystical character which is lasting, indestructible, powerful and irresistible. Thus the high priest presiding at Tantrik Rites is called Dorje Lopon. In fact, diamond is so called because of the hard character of this gem. In the Indian Tantrik worship, Vajra occurs as in Vajrapushpa (Vajra-flower), Vajra-bhumi (Vajra-ground), and so forth, but these are not "diamond" flowers or earth. An extremely interesting inquiry is here opened which is beyond the scope of this Chapter, for the term Vajra, which is again the appellation of this particular school (Vajrayana), and is of great significance in the history of that power-side of religion which is dealt with in the *Shakta Tantra*. (See *Introduction to Shri-Cakra-Samb-hara*.)

(Here, without further attempt at explanation, I keep the term Vajra adding only that Harinisa is not, as has been thought, Vajra-Varahi (Dorje-phagmo) Herself but the Bija Mantras (Ha, ri, ni, sa) of Her four attendant Dakinis.)

Vajra-Sattva and Vajrapani, Buddha and Bodhisattva of the Vajrayana faith transformed themselves into the forms of Haya-griva and Vajra-Varahi, and assumed the costumes of Herukas.

(The Herukas are a class of Vajrayana Devatas, of half terrible features, represented as partly nude with an upper garment of human skin and tiger skin round the loins. They have a skull head-dress, carry bone rosaries, a staff and Damaru like Shiva. The Herukas are described in the Tibetan books as being beautiful, heroic, awe-inspiring, stern and majestic.) Blazing in the nine kinds of physical magnificence and splendor, they proceeded to the Malaya Mountain—the abode of the Rutra. On the four sides of the Mountain were four gates. Each gate was guarded by a Demoness, bearing respectively a Mare's, Sow's, Lion's and a Dog's head. These the Glorious One conquered, and united therewith in a spirit of nonattachment. From their union were born the following female issue: (1) The White Horse-faced, (2) The Black Sow-faced, (3) The Red Lion-faced, (4) and the Green Dog-faced daughters. Proceeding still further He met another cordon of sentries, who too were females, bearing the heads of (1) Lioness, (2) Tigress, (3) Fox, (4) Wolf, (5) Vulture, (6) Kaṅka, (7) Raven, and (8) Owl. With these Demonesses too, the Glorious One united in a spirit of non-attachment, and blessed the act. Of this union were born female offspring, each of whom took after the mother in outward shape or Matter, and after the father in Mind. Thus were the eight Demi-goddesses born: *viz.,* the Lion-headed, Tiger-headed and so forth. Being divine in mind, they possess prescience and wisdom, although from their mother they retained their shape and features, which are those of brutes.

Then again proceeding further inward, He came upon the daughters of the Rutras and of Rakshasas, named respectively, Nyobyed-ma or "She who maddens," Tagbyed-ma "She who frightens," Dri-medma "The unsullied," Kem-pama "She who dries one up," Phorthogma "She who bears the Cup," and Zhyongthogma the "bowl bearer."

The Glorious One united with these in the same manner, and from them, were born the eight Matrikas of the eight Sthanas (sacred places), known as Gaurima and so forth. These, too, possessed divine wisdom from their father and terrific features and shapes from their mothers.

(There are 24 Sthanas which are places of pilgrimage and eight great cemeteries making 32 in all. In each of these cemeteries there is a powerful Goddess also called Mamo, that is, Matrika. These terrible Goddesses are, according to the Zhi-Khro, Gaurima, Tsaurima, Candali, Vetali, Gasmari, Shonama, Pramo, Puskasi. These are in color white, yellow, yellowish white, black, dark green, dark blue, red, reddish yellow, and are situated in the East, South, N.W., North, S.W., N.E., West, S.E., "nerve-leafs of the conch-shell mansion" (brain) respectively. These are the eight great Matrikas of the eight great Cemeteries, to whom prayer is made, that when forms are changed and entrance is made on the intermediate plane ("The Bardo" / Cf. *The Tibetan Book of the Dead),* they may place the spirit on the clear light path of Radiance (Hodsal).)

(These complementarily denote the union of Divine Mind with gross matter. In working with matter the Divine mind is always detached. Work is possible even for the liberated consciousness when free from attachment, that is, desire (Kama), which is bondage. The Divine Mind unites with terrible forms of gross matter that these may be instruments; in this case instruments whereby the gross Egoism of the Rutra is to be subdued.)

Then, going right into the innermost abode, he found that the Rutra had gone out in search of food, which consisted of human flesh and of Devas. Adopting the disguise of the Rutra, the Glorious One went in to the Consort of the Rutra, the Rakshasi-Queen Krodheshvari (Lady of Wrath) in the same spirit as before, and blessed the act. By Krodheshvari, He had male issue, Bhagavan Vajra-Keruka, with three faces and six hands, terrific to behold. Then the Glorious One, Hayagriva, and his divine Consort, Vajra-Varahi, each expressed their triumph by neighing and grunting thrice. Upon hearing these sounds the Rutra was struck with mortal fear, and coming to the spot, he said:

"What sayest Thou, little son of Hayagriva and Vajra-Varahi.
All the world of Devas and Asuras
Proclaim my virtues and sing my praises.
I cannot be conquered. Rest yourselves in peace,
Regard me with humility, and bow down to me.
Even the Regent of the Devas, of the odd garment (priestly dress),
Failed to conquer me in days of yore."

Saying this, he raised his hands and came to lay them on the young one's head. Thereupon, Hayagriva at once entered the body of the Rutra by the secret path (Guhya) from below and piercing him right through from below upwards, He showed His Horse's Head, on the top of the head of the Rutra. The oily fat of the Rutra's body made the Horse's head look green. The mane, dyed with blood, became red, and the eye-brows, having been splashed with the bile of the Demon, became yellow. The forehead, being splashed with the brains, became white. Thus the Glorious One, having assumed the shape and dresses of the Rutra, took on a terrible majesty.

At the same time, Vajra-Varahi, His Consort, also entered the body of the Rutra's Consort Krodheshvari, in the same manner piercing and impaling her. She forced Her own Sow's head right up through the crown of the Demoness' head, until it towered above it. The Sow's head had assumed a black color, from having been steeped in the fat of the Rakshasi. Then the two Divine Beings embraced each other, and begot an offspring, a Divine Being, a male of the Terrific Order, a Krodhabhairava. Having done this, Hayagriva neighed shrilly six times, and Vajra-Varahi grunted deeply five times. Then the hosts of the Buddhas and the Bodhisattvas assembled there as thickly as birds of prey settling down on carrion. They filled all space. They were of the peaceful, the wrathful, the half-peaceful and the half-wrathful orders, in inconceivably large numbers. They began to surround the Rutra-Tharpa-Nagpo, who, being unable to bear the pain of being stretched asunder, cried in agony:

"Oh, I am defeated!

The Horse and the Sow have defeated the Rutra.

The Buddhas have defeated the Demons.

Religion has conquered Ir-religion,

The Sangha has defeated the Tirthikas.

Indra has defeated the Asuras,

The Asuras have defeated the Moon,

The Garuda has defeated the Ocean,

Fire defeats fuel, Wind scatters the Clouds,

Diamond (Vajra) pierces metals.

Oh! It was I who said

    that last night's dream portended evil.

Oh! Slay me quick,

    if you are going to slay me."

As he said this, his bowels were involuntarily loosened, and from the excreta which, being thus purified, fell into the Ocean, there at once arose a precious sandal tree, which was a wish-granting tree. This tree struck its root in the nether world of the Serpent-spirits, spread its foliage in the Asura-lokas, and bore its fruits in the Deva-lokas. And the fruits were named Amrita (the essence and elixir of life).

Then the two Chief Actor and Actress, Hayagriva and Vajra-Varahi acted the joyful plays called the 'Plays of Happy Cause,' 'Happy Path', and 'Happy Result', in the nine glorious measures.

(That is, plays in which the actors are happy being the male and female Divinities, in this case Hayagriva and Vajra-Varahi. They are the cause; their play being exoterically "Dalliance" (Lila, and their result the dispelling of Egoism which is Illumination.))

Just as a victor in a battle, who has slain his enemy, wins the armor and the accoutrements of his slain opponent, and puts them on as a sign of triumph, so also, the Glorious One having conquered the Rutra, assumed the eight accoutrements of the foe, including the wings, and the other adornments which made him look so bright and magnificent. These the Glorious One blessed and consecrated to the use of the Divine Deities. Having done all this, both Hayagriva and Vajra-Varahi returned to the Realm of pure Spiritual Being (Dharmadhatu). Thus it comes about that those costumes, assumed by the Rutra, came to be adopted as the attire of the Deities. Their having three heads, the eight sepulchral ornaments, and the eight glorious costumes and wings, had origin in this event.

Then Pal Chag-na-dorje (Shri Vajrapani) multiplied himself into countless Avataras, and these again multiplied themselves into myriads of Avataras, all of the terrible and wrathful type. The Rutra too showed supernatural powers, for he transformed himself into a nine-headed Monster, having eighteen hands, as huge as the Mount Meru. Should it be doubted, how this sinful being could still possess such supernatural powers, one must know that he was a Bodhisattva of the eighth degree (one who has attained eight Bhumikas or stages of advance out of thirteen) who had fallen back. Hence was it, that even the Buddhas found it difficult to subdue him, not to count the world of Devas and men. Then Vajrapani manifested still greater divine powers of every imaginable description, and all the Buddhas and Bodhisattvas fixed their abodes on the greatly enlarged and distended body of the Rutra. The latter, unable to bear the agony of this pressure, roared with pain:

> "Come quick to the rescue, O my followers, who inhabit the
>   ten directions
> To the right and left of the Skull-like Mansion
> And those who live in the gardens and the orchards.
> Yakshas, Rakshasas, and Pretas millions in number,
>   advance to the rescue at once.
> O, ye followers and adherents of the Rutra, who dwell in
>   the twenty-four places, and countries
> Numbering millions and tens of millions, who have sworn
>   allegiance to me
> And promised to serve me faithfully, and ye from the
>   illimitable spaces in every direction
> Fill the heavens and the earth with your innumerable
>   hosts and all in one body strike (at the foe) with the
>   weapons in your hands, sounding the battle cry
>   'Om-rulu-rulu.'"

Though he uttered these commands, there was none to obey him. Everyone surrendered to Bhagavan Vajra-Heruka. Thus all the subordinates of the Rutra, the thirty-two Dakinis, the seven Matrikas, and the four "Sisters," (Sringbzhi), the eight Furies (Barmas or flaming ones), the eight Genii (spirits or attendants on the Devatas) and the sixty-four Messengers all came over to the Heruka and the Divine offspring (the Krodha-Bhairava) took upon himself the duty of serving the food of the Deities.

(This is the Deity usually invoked for purification and religious contrition; it is seen that his undertaking to serve the food of the Deities means purifying and absolving the sins of the Rutra.)

Vajrapani, producing ten divine beings of the terrific type (Krodhabhairava), gave a Phurpa (triangular-shaped dagger) to each of them, and commanded them to go and destroy the Rutra and his party. Thereupon Hayagriva came again, and neighed three times; upon hearing which sound, the entire host of the Rutra were seized with a panic and all were subdued. Then "Black Salvation" (Tharpa-Nagpo) and his followers were rendered powerless and helpless: humbled and quite submissive. So they surrendered their own homes, personal ornaments, and lives, and uttered these words of entreaty:

"Obeisance to Thee, O, Thou field of the Buddhas' influence,

Obeisance to Thee, O, Thou who dost cause Karma to bear fruit.

I and all of us having sown previous evil Karma

Are now reaping the fruits thereof, which all indeed may see.

Our future depends on what we have done now;

Karma follows us, as inexorably as the shadow does the body.

Everyone must taste the fruit of what each has himself done.

Even should one repent, and be sorry for his deeds

There is no help for him as Karma cannot be avoided.

So we who are destined by Karma to drink the bitter cup to the very dregs,

We do therefore offer up our bodies to serve as the cushion of Thy footstool.

Pray accept them as such."

Having said so, they laid themselves prostrate, and from this originates the symbolism of every Deity having a Rutra underneath his feet. Then the vassal Chiefs of the Rutra submitted their prayers:

"We have no claim to sit in the middle, Be pleased to place us at the extremities of the Mandalas. We have no right to demand of the best of the banquets. We pray to be favored with the leavings, and the dregs of food and drink. Henceforth, we are Your subjects, and will never disobey Your commands. We will obey You in whatever You are pleased to command. As a loving mother is attracted towards her son, So shall we, too, be surely drawn near those who remind us of this oath of allegiance."

Thus did they take the oath of allegiance. Then the Holder of the Mysteries, the Glorious One—Vajrapani, pierced the heart of the prostrate Rutra with the Phurpa dagger and absolved him. All his Karmik sins and his Passions (Klesha) were thus immediately absolved. Then power was conferred on him, and vows were laid on him, and the water of Faith was poured on him. His body, speech and mind were blessed and consecrated towards Divine Service, and the Dorje of Faith was laid on the head, throat and heart. Thenceforward he was empowered to be the Guardian of the Faith, and named the Good Dark One, and his secret name conferred at the Initiation was Mahakala. Thus was he included in the assembly of the Vajrayana Deities. Finally, it was revealed to him that he would become a Buddha, by the name of Thalwai-Wangpo (the Lord of Ashes) in the World called Kod-pa-lhundrup (that is "self-produced" or "made-all-at-once"). Then the Rutra's dead body was thrown on this Jambu-dvipa, where it fell on its back. The head fell on Sinhala (Ceylon), the right arm and hand upon Thogar and the left hand on Le (Ladak country). The right leg fell on Nepal, and the left on Kashmir. The entrails fell over Zahor. The heart fell on Urgyen (Cabul), and the Linga on Magadha. These form the eight chief countries. Thus the eight Matrikas of the eight Sthanas, headed by Gaurima and others: the eight natural Stupas headed by Potala; the eight occult Powers, which fascinate; the eight guardians (female), who ench-ant; the eight great trees, the eight great realm-protectors (Shing-kyong), the eight lakes, the eight great Naga spirits, the eight clouds, and the eight great Dikpalas (Cyogs-kyong or Protectors of the Directions) as well as the eight great cemeteries originated.

With the end of the sixth Chapter of the *Golden Rosary* is con-cluded the account of the Vajrayana Devatas who appeared to aid in the conquest of human Egoism which had manifested itself in terrible form in the person of the great Rutra. As all but the fully pure have in them Rutra elements, they are enjoined in Vajrayana to follow the methods of expurgation there revealed.

Annotations

Rather than using superscripted numbers in the main text, the main text lacks superscripts, and each annotation in this context is part of the publisher's choice of a sample of perspectives that a beholder could find relevant as commentary on elements of portions and/or elements of the whole.

"The Tâo that can be trodden is not the enduring and unchanging Tâo. The name that can be named is not the enduring and unchanging name."
    —Lao-Tzu, the First Verse of Chapter One of *The Tao Te Ching*, as translated by James Legge

"All that we are is the result of what we have thought: it is founded on our thoughts, it is made up of our thoughts. If a man speaks or acts with an evil thought, pain follows him, as the wheel follows the foot of the ox that draws the carriage."
    —Unknown/Anonymous Author(s) (thought to be Shakyamuni Buddha and/or another member and/or other members of the early sangha), the opening lines of Chapter One of *The Dhammapada*, as translated by F. Max Müller

"The evil-doer suffers in this world, and he suffers in the next; he suffers in both. He suffers when he thinks of the evil he has done; he suffers more when going on the evil path."
    —Unknown/Anonymous Author(s), Verse 17 of Chapter One of *The Dhammapada*, as translated by F. Max Müller

"The virtuous man delights in this world, and he delights in the next; he delights in both. He delights and rejoices, when he sees the purity of his own work."
    —Unknown/Anonymous Author(s), Verse 16 of Chapter One of *The Dhammapada*, as translated by F. Max Müller

"He who stands on his tiptoes does not stand firm; he who stretches his legs does not walk (easily). (So), he who displays himself does not shine; he who asserts his own views is not distinguished; he who vaunts himself does not find his merit acknowledged; he who is self-conceited has no superiority allowed to him. Such conditions, viewed from the standpoint of the Tâo, are like remnants of food, or a tumour on the body, which all dislike. Hence those who pursue (the course) of the Tâo do not adopt and allow them."

—Lao-Tzu, Chapter 24 of *The Tao Te Ching*, as translated by James Legge

"Consider all nations and empires that have ever risen and fallen, and how it is that some of them more closely paralleled the rise and fall of Matam Rutra than did others."

—Synapsid Revelations Press, composed on December 21, 2024 specifically for inclusion in this book (As of the time of going to publication with this work, it is unknown to the publisher whether this had appeared in any prior publication(s), though the quote's simplicity means that it might have done that.)

"Form is emptiness, and emptiness indeed is form. Emptiness is not different from form, form is not different from emptiness. What is form that is emptiness, what is emptiness that is form."

—The Unknown Author(s) of *The Larger Prajnaparamita-Hridaya Sutra*, as translated by F. Max Müller / {within that, as part of a quote attributed to Aryavalokitesvara}

"The virtuous man is happy in this world, and he is happy in the next; he is happy in both. He is happy when he thinks of the good he has done; he is still more happy when going on the good path."

—Unknown/Anonymous Author(s), Verse 18 of Chapter One of *The Dhammapada*, as translated by F. Max Müller

"There are the five Skandhas, and these he considered as by their nature empty (phenomenal)."

—The Unknown Author(s) of *The Smaller Prajnaparamita-Hridaya Sutra*, as translated by F. Max Müller

"Heaven is long-enduring and earth continues long. The reason why heaven and earth are able to endure and continue thus long is because they do not live of, or for, themselves. This is how they are able to continue and endure."

—Lao-Tzu, Verse One of Chapter Seven of *The Tao Te Ching*, as translated by James Legge

"They who know truth in truth, and untruth in untruth, arrive at truth, and follow true desires."

—Unknown/Anonymous Author(s), Verse 12 of Chapter One of *The Dhammapada*, as translated by F. Max Müller

"Therefore the sage puts his own person last, and yet it is found in the foremost place; he treats his person as if it were foreign to him, and yet that person is preserved. Is it not because he has no personal and private ends, that therefore such ends are realized?"

—Lao-Tzu, Verse Two of Chapter Seven of *The Tao Te Ching*, as translated by James Legge

"What do you think then, O Subhûti, has the highest perfect knowledge been known to the Tathâgata through the possession of signs? You should not think so, O Subhûti. And why? Because, O Subhûti, the highest perfect knowledge would not be known by the Tathâgata through the possession of signs. Nor should anybody, O Subhûti, say to you that the destruction or annihilation of any thing is proclaimed by those who have entered on the path of the Bodhisattvas."

—The Unknown Author(s) of *The Vajrachedika* (also known as *The Diamond Sutra* or *The Diamond Cutter*), as translated by F. Max Müller

"Therefore he who would administer the kingdom, honouring it as he honours his own person, may be employed to govern it, and he who would administer it with the love which he bears to his own person may be entrusted with it."

—Lao-Tzu, Verse Three of Chapter 13 of *The Tao Te Ching*, as translated by James Legge

*   *   *   *   *   *   *   *   *   *

"Here is a list of nations, continents, other places, and periods, and perhaps someone might want to do the math, the social psychology, and the military science: Sumer, Ancient Times; China, Ancient Times; Elsewhere, Ancient Times; India, the Second Millennium; North America, the Second Millennium; Europe, the Twentieth Century; Asia, the Twenty-First Century; Africa, the Twenty-First Century, North America, the Third Millennium, Everywhere on Earth, the Third Millennium; Space, From This Instant Onward."

—Synapsid Revelations Press, composed on December 21, 2024 specifically for inclusion in this book (As of the time of going to publication with this work, it is unknown to the publisher whether this had appeared in any prior publication(s), though theoretically it might have.)

*   *   *   *   *   *   *   *   *   *

"Thus, O Sâriputra, all things have the character of emptiness, they have no beginning, no end, they are faultless and not faultless, they are not imperfect and not perfect."

—The Unknown Author(s) of *The Larger Prajnaparamita-Hridaya Sutra*, as translated by F. Max Müller / {within that, as part of a quote attributed to Aryavalokitesvara}

*   *   *   *   *   *   *   *   *   *

THREE MORE QUOTATIONS TO CONSIDER:

"Men come forth and live; they enter (again) and die. Of every ten three are ministers of life (to themselves); and three are ministers of death. There are also three in every ten whose aim is to live, but whose movements tend to the land (or place) of death. And for what reason? Because of their excessive endeavours to perpetuate life. But I have heard that he who is skilful in managing the life entrusted to him for a time travels on the land without having to shun rhinoceros or tiger, and enters a host without having to avoid buff coat or sharp weapon. The rhinoceros finds no place in him into which to thrust its horn, nor the tiger a place in which to fix its claws, nor the weapon a place to admit its point. And for what reason? Because there is in him no place of death." —Chapter Fifty of *The Tao Te Ching*, circa the 5th or 6th century B.C.E., by Lao-Tzu, as translated in the 19th century C.E. by James Legge

"If your interpretation of anyone or anything causes you to hate, then you might be cruising for a bruising." —Synapsid Revelations Press, composed on December 20, 2024 specifically for inclusion in this book (As of the time of going to publication with this work, it is unknown to the publisher whether this had appeared in any prior publication(s), though the quote's simplicity means that it might have done that.)

"For hatred does not cease by hatred at any time: hatred ceases by love, this is an old rule." —*The Dhammapada*, Chapter One, Verse Five; of circa the 5th or 6th century B.C.E., translated this way in the 19th century C.E. by F. Max Müller / Note that according to legend, the Anonymous/Unknown Author(s) of that work may have been a member or multiple members of the early sangha. Some versions of the legend attribute it to Shakyamuni Buddha.

www.ingramcontent.com/pod-product-compliance
Lightning Source LLC
Chambersburg PA
CBHW060956120626
46557CB00003B/1193